ZAP the Nags, Embrace Your Swags!

Marcy Schaaf

Hello there, superstar!

Did you know you're one-of-a-kind?
That's right—there's no one else like YOU in the whole wide world! You were born with a special gift, something that makes you shine brighter than the stars. But sometimes, those pesky little thoughts called "nags" try to trick us into forgetting how amazing we are.
This book is here to help you zap those nags and discover the incredible gift that's already inside you. Whether you love to build, create, help, or dream, your talent is your superpower, and the world needs it!
So get ready for a fun and inspiring journey.

By the end of this book, you'll know how to turn off the doubts and turn up your light.

Let's show the world just how unstoppable you are!
With big smiles and even bigger dreams!

Oh no! Oh dear!
What's that I hear?
"Your hair's a mess,
my little peer!"

"Too short, too tall,
too slow, too small."
Those nasty nags
can ruin it all!

Each day they come,
they sneak;
they creep—
57,000 before we
sleep!

These nags are sly,
they love to tease,
"Don't try,"
they say,
"Just sit at ease."

But hold on now,
don't let them win,
Those pesky nags
don't live within!

They're noisy whispers,
not the truth,
They try to spoil your best of youth!

Did you know, deep in your heart,
You've had a gift right from the start?

Some can teach,
and some can bake,
Some can build,
and some create!

These gifts were planted, just for you,
To grow and shine in all you do.

"But how?" you ask. "I cannot see,
What gift on Earth belongs to me?"

Don't fret, don't frown,
don't make a fuss,
Your gift is there—just wait,
just trust!

It's what you love,
it's what feels right,
It's what you'd do
both day and night.

Maybe you'll paint or write a rhyme,
Or help a friend who's out of time.

But wait!

There's more—did you know this?
Your gift will lead to joy and bliss!

The nags will shout,
"You'll never do!"
But here's the trick:
keep being YOU!

If nags pop in to make you doubt,
Go build, go run, go dance, get out!

Productivity's the trick,
you see,
It keeps those nags
from bothering me!

"Create, explore, give love,"
I say,
And chase the pesky nags away!

They hate to see you
busy and bright,
They shrink away,
they take to flight!

When you're building,
or learning,
or making new friends,
The nags stay away—
your joy never ends!

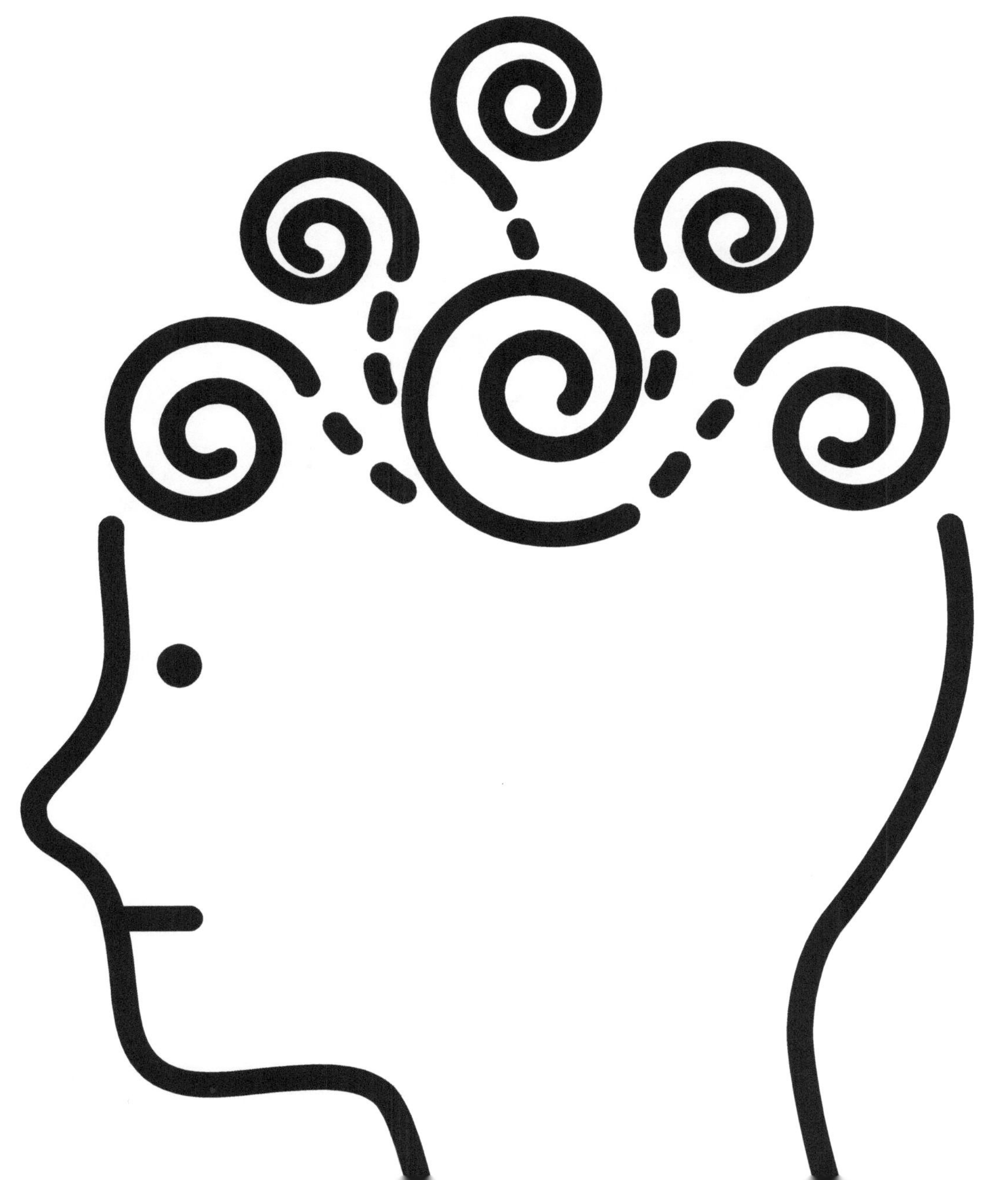

So when they whisper,
"You're not enough!"
Just shout right back,
"That's silly stuff!"

"Because I've got gifts,
and I've got dreams,
I'm building my kingdom with bright,
shiny beams!"

And if you don't believe
in gifts from above,
Just think of the things
you already love.

From math
to sports
to baking a pie,
Your talents and gifts will help you fly!

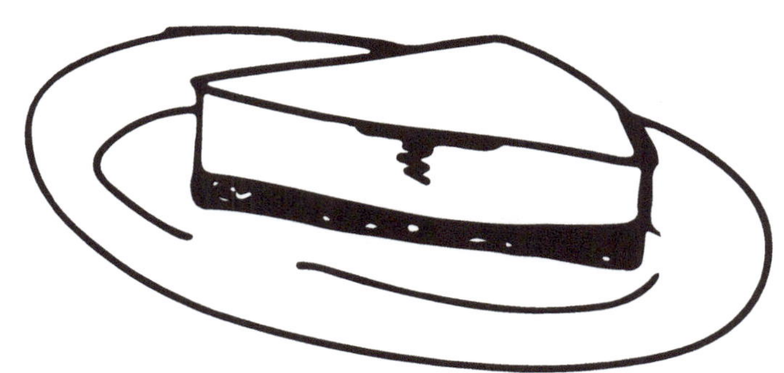

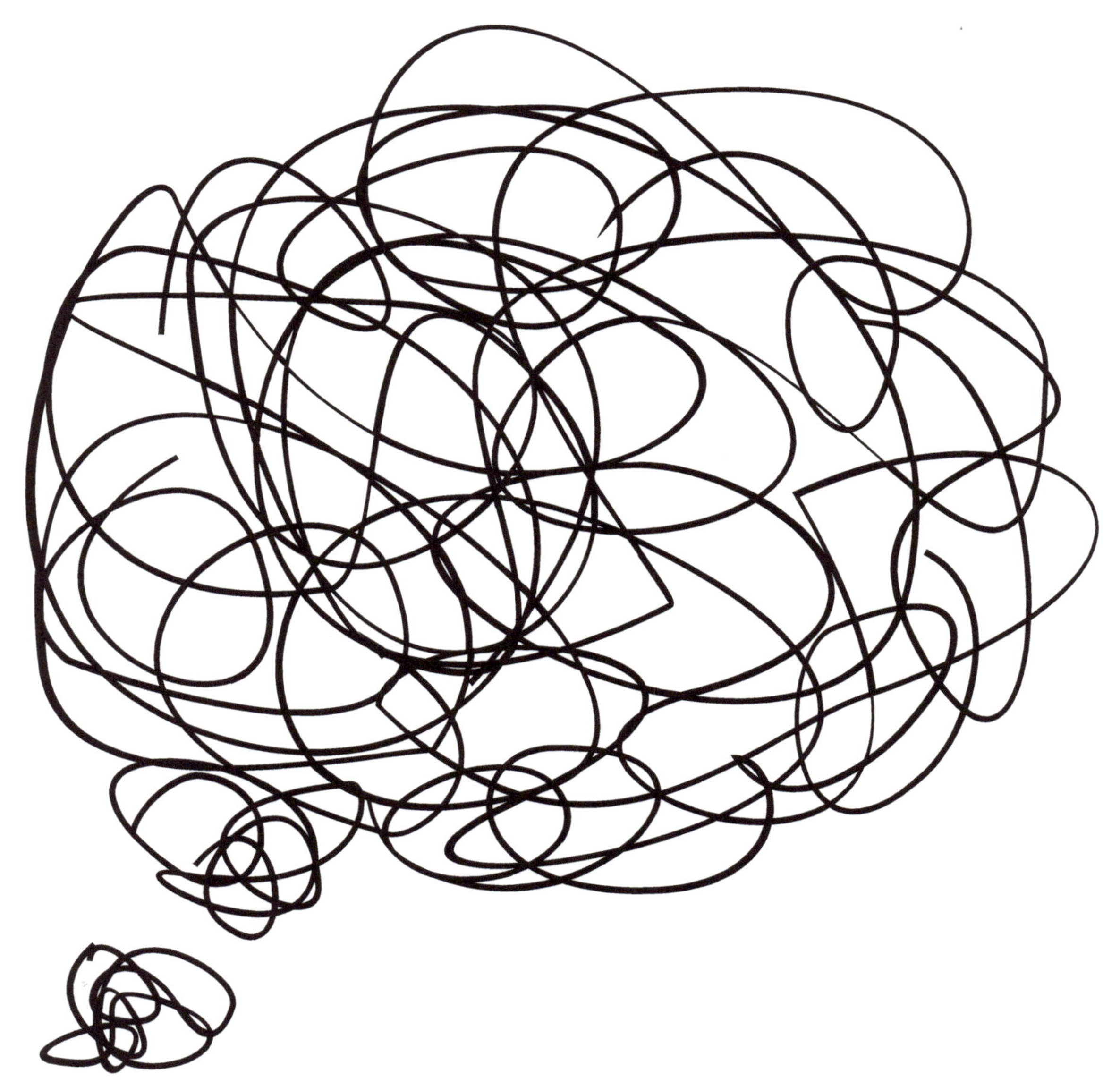

So build, create,
and soon you'll see,
The nags don't stand a chance,
not with me!

Because we're born to teach,
to build, to make,
And fill the world with joy we stake!

So go ahead,
ignore the nags,
And shine with gifts
in all your

Your talent's here;
it's in your heart,
So show the world
your shining part!

And when you doubt, just look inside
Your gift's your compass,
your guide, your pride!

So chase your dreams,
no need to fear,
Your gift will shine year after year!

Join Our Book of the Month Club!

Looking for the perfect gift that keeps on giving? Join our Book of the Month Club! For just $25 a month, or $250 if you purchase a year upfront, you or your loved ones will receive a handpicked children's book every month, straight to your doorstep.

Here's how it works:
Choose from 15 different languages to receive bilingual books that make learning fun.
Enjoy monthly shipments of our exclusive books that inspire, teach, and entertain children of all ages.
Each month's book is carefully selected to provide a new adventure, valuable lesson, and a chance to explore cultures from around the world.
It's the perfect gift for birthdays, holidays, or just because! Whether you're nurturing a young reader or encouraging language learning, our Book of the Month Club is designed to bring joy to every bookshelf.

Exclusive Bonus: As part of your membership, you'll also receive a monthly podcast about our featured book delivered straight to your email! Listen in for behind-the-scenes insights, fun facts, and tips for making storytime even more magical.

Sign up today at www.Booksbyschaaf.com and start enjoying the gift of reading all year long!

Books By Schaaf

www.BookBySchaaf.com

Podcast series about our book on TikTok.

Activity Guide companion's for each storybook can be found on our website.

Find us at: